SUPER SIMPLE
BACKYARD
CRITTER CRAFTS

Fun and Easy Animal Crafts

Sammy Bosch

Consulting Editor, Diane Craig, M.A./Reading Specialist

Super Sandcastle

An Imprint of Abdo Publishing
abdopublishing.com

abdopublishing.com

Published by Abdo Publishing, a division of ABDO, PO Box 398166, Minneapolis, Minnesota 55439. Copyright © 2017 by Abdo Consulting Group, Inc. International copyrights reserved in all countries. No part of this book may be reproduced in any form without written permission from the publisher. Super SandCastle™ is a trademark and logo of Abdo Publishing.

Printed in the United States of America, North Mankato, Minnesota
062016
092016

THIS BOOK CONTAINS
RECYCLED MATERIALS

Editor: Liz Salzmann
Content Developer: Nancy Tuminelly
Craft Production: Frankie Tuminelly
Cover and Interior Design and Production: Colleen Dolphin, Mighty Media, Inc.
Photo Credits: Mighty Media, Inc.; Shutterstock
The following manufacturers/names appearing in this book are trademarks:
Americana®, Elmer's® Glue-All®

Library of Congress Cataloging-in-Publication Data
Names: Bosch, Sammy, author.
Title: Super simple backyard critter crafts : fun and easy animal crafts / by Sammy Bosch ; consulting editor, Diane Craig, M.A./Reading Specialist.
Other titles: Backyard critter crafts
Description: Minneapolis, Minnesota : Abdo Publishing, [2017] | Series: Super simple critter crafts
Identifiers: LCCN 2016001414 (print) | LCCN 2016004600 (ebook) | ISBN 9781680781601 (print) | ISBN 9781680776034 (ebook)
Subjects: LCSH: Handicraft--Juvenile literature. | Suburban animals--Juvenile literature.
Classification: LCC TT160 .B757 2017 (print) | LCC TT160 (ebook) | DDC 745.59--dc23
LC record available at http://lccn.loc.gov/2016001414

Super SandCastle™ books are created by a team of professional educators, reading specialists, and content developers around five essential components— phonemic awareness, phonics, vocabulary, text comprehension, and fluency—to assist young readers as they develop reading skills and strategies and increase their general knowledge. All books are written, reviewed, and leveled for guided reading and early reading intervention programs for use in shared, guided, and independent reading and writing activities to support a balanced approach to literacy instruction.

TO ADULT HELPERS

The craft projects in this series are fun and simple. There are just a few things to remember to keep kids safe. Some projects require the use of sharp or hot objects. Also, kids may be using messy materials such as glue or paint. Make sure they protect their clothes and work surfaces. Review the projects before starting, and be ready to assist when necessary.

KEY SYMBOL

Watch for this warning symbol in this book. Here is what it means.

 HOT!
You will be working with something hot. Get help from an adult!

CONTENTS

BACKYARD CRITTERS

Parks and playgrounds are fun places to explore. So is your backyard!

Your yard has many different critters. Some are on the ground. Others are high in the trees. It is fun to watch and learn about them.

What critters are in your yard? Make some cute crafts about them and other backyard critters.

GET TO KNOW YOUR BACKYARD!

FUN FACTS ABOUT ANIMALS AND INSECTS IN YOUR BACKYARD

RABBITS

Rabbits are great jumpers. A rabbit can jump 36 inches (91 cm) high!

BIRDS

The American robin is a common backyard bird. A robin's egg is blue.

LADYBUGS

A **ladybug**'s spots and bright color warn off predators.

GRASSHOPPERS

Grasshoppers are musicians! They can make noise by rubbing their hind legs against their wings.

SQUIRRELS

Squirrels **hibernate** in winter. But they sometimes wake up to find and eat food they have stored.

Bees

Honeybees are the only insects that produce food for humans.

CHIPMUNKS

Chipmunks stuff their cheeks with food to carry back to their nests.

BUTTERFLIES

Butterflies taste with their feet! They also use their feet to find good leaves to lay eggs on.

7

MAKE A CRITTER-FRIENDLY BACKYARD!

WAYS TO HELP BACKYARD CRITTERS SURVIVE

HEARTY GARDEN

Rabbits need fresh vegetables. Plant lettuce, carrots, and other vegetables for them to eat.

HEALTHY GRASS

Backyard animals spend a lot of time in the grass. Use natural **fertilizers** and weed control products. These products won't harm your backyard critters.

BIRD FEEDERS & BIRDBATHS

Birds need food and water too. Put a birdbath and bird feeder in your yard. Be sure to keep them filled.

FLOWERS

Bees and **butterflies** need pollen from flowers to survive. Plant many different kinds of flowers in your yard for these insects.

9

MATERIALS

HERE ARE SOME OF THE THINGS YOU'LL NEED TO DO THE PROJECTS.

acrylic paint

can

card stock

chenille stems

clothespins

craft glue

egg carton

felt

googly eyes

hot glue gun & glue sticks

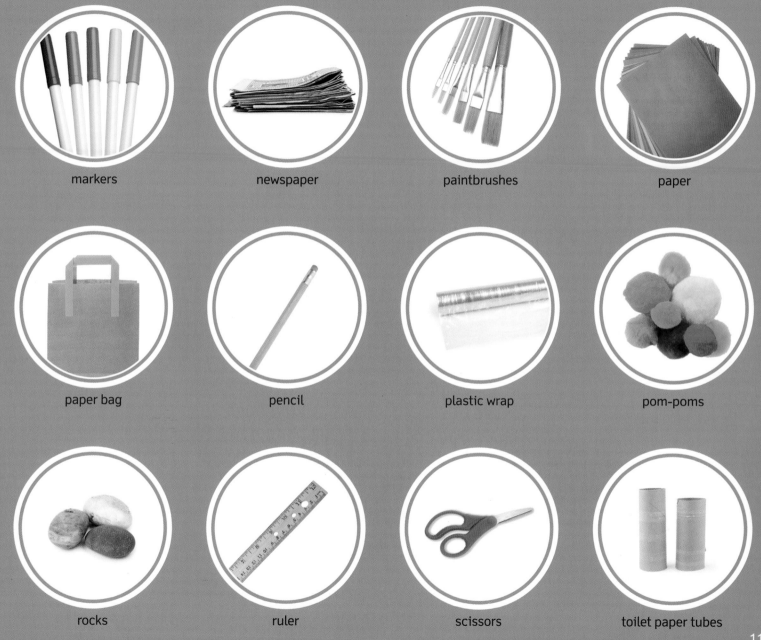

markers

newspaper

paintbrushes

paper

paper bag

pencil

plastic wrap

pom-poms

rocks

ruler

scissors

toilet paper tubes

11

BASHFUL BUNNY BUDDIES

YOU'LL BE SO "HOPPY" TO MAKE THESE CUTE BUNNIES!

white paper   ruler   green paper   pink marker

scissors   craft glue   googly eyes

1. Cut a strip of white paper. Make it 1 by 4 inches (2.5 by 10 cm). Glue the ends together to form a circle. This is the bunny's head.

2. Cut two more strips of white paper for the legs. Make each one ½ by 3 inches (1.3 cm by 7.5 cm). Fold the ends of each strip to make feet.

3. Cut a rectangle out of green paper. This will be the grass the bunny sits on. Glue the feet to the green paper so that the legs make arches. Glue the head on top of the legs.

4. Draw ears on white paper and cut them out. Fold the base of the ears and glue the fold to the head.

5. Glue googly eyes to the front of the head. Draw a pink nose and mouth.

6. Cut another rectangle out of green paper. It should be slightly shorter than the first green rectangle. Cut thin triangles along one long side. Fold the other side slightly to make grass that stands up. Glue it next to the bunny.

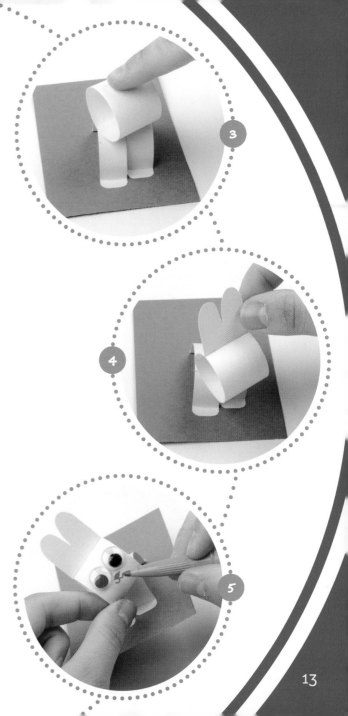

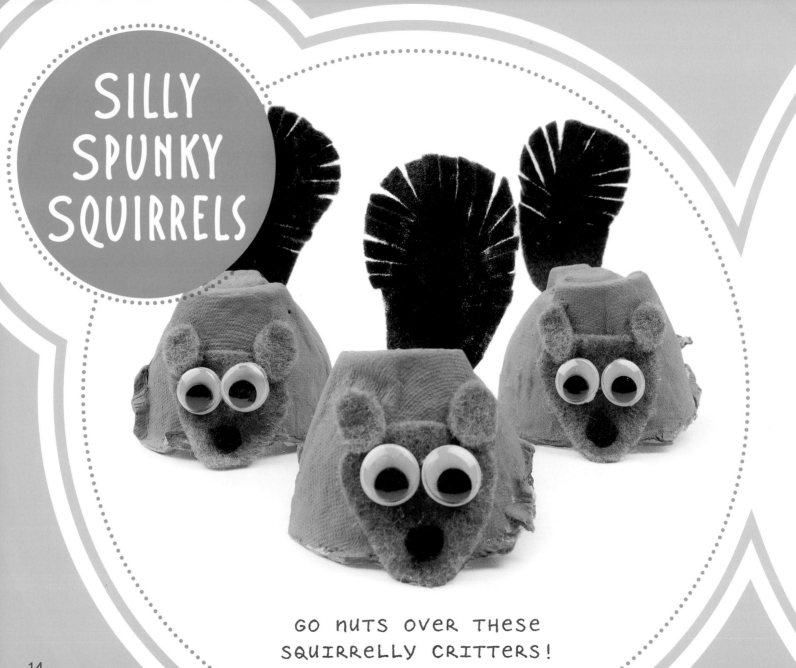

SILLY SPUNKY SQUIRRELS

GO NUTS OVER THESE SQUIRRELLY CRITTERS!

MATERIALS 🔥

newspaper	light brown felt	googly eyes
egg carton	ruler	small black pom-pom
brown paint	scissors	dark brown felt
paintbrush	hot glue gun & glue sticks	brown chenille stem
pencil		

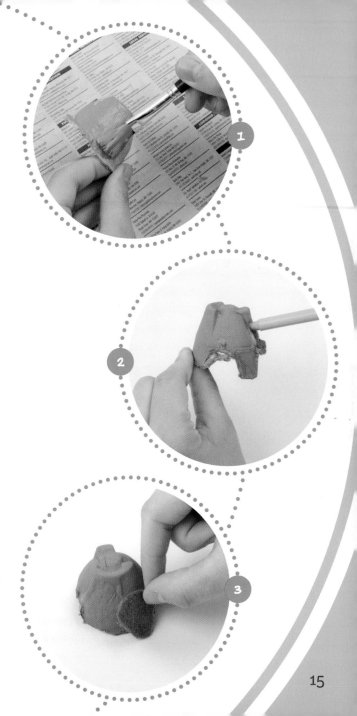

1. Cover your work surface with newspaper. Cut a cup off the egg carton. Paint the egg carton cup brown. Let it dry.

2. Poke a hole in the side of the cup with the pencil.

3. Cut a rounded triangle out of light brown felt. Make it about 1 inch (2.5 cm) wide. Hot glue the wide end of the triangle to the side of the cup. Put it opposite the hole you created. This is the squirrel's face.

(continued on next page)

4   Cut two small ovals out of light brown felt. Hot glue them above the face for ears.

5   Glue two googly eyes on the face.

6   Glue the small pom-pom below the eyes for the nose.

7. Cut a teardrop shape out of dark brown felt. Make it about 2 inches (5 cm) long. Make small cuts around the edges of the teardrop. This is the squirrel's tail.

8. Cut a 3½-inch (9 cm) piece of chenille stem. Hot glue the stem to the tail.

9. Stick the other end of the stem through the hole in the cup. Bend the chenille stem so the tail sticks up.

10. Set this silly squirrel on display! Then make more squirrels out of the other egg carton cups.

NEST FOR THREE

A ROBIN'S NEST
WITHIN REACH!

MATERIALS

brown paper bag	plastic wrap	light blue paint
scissors	craft glue	paintbrush
newspaper	spoon	
2 bowls	3 oval rocks	

1. Cut the paper bag into small strips.

2. Cover your work surface with newspaper. Turn a bowl upside down. Cover it with plastic wrap. Put equal amounts of glue and water in the other bowl. Stir them together.

3. Dip the paper bag strips in the glue. Lay them on the upside-down bowl. Cover the entire bowl with paper strips. Add dry strips on top. Let it dry for 48 hours.

4. When the glue is dry, remove the nest from the bowl. Carefully peel off the plastic wrap.

5. Paint the three rocks blue. Let them dry. Place the eggs in the nest.

THESE HAPPY BEES
DON'T STING!

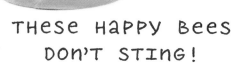

MATERIALS 🔥

newspaper
toilet paper tube
yellow paint
paintbrush
black paint

yellow paper
ruler
pencil
scissors
black marker

1 black chenille stem
hot glue gun
 & glue sticks
white paper

1. Cover your work surface with newspaper. Paint the toilet paper tube yellow. Let it dry.

2. Paint three black stripes around the tube. Let it dry.

3. Draw a 1-inch (2.5 cm) circle on yellow paper. Cut the circle out.

(continued on next page)

4 Draw eyes and a mouth on the circle with black marker.

5 Cut two 2-inch (5 cm) pieces of black chenille stem.

6 Roll one end of each stem into a ball.

7 Hot glue the other end of each stem to the back of the face.

8   Hot glue the face to one end of the tube.

9   Cut two ovals out of white paper. Make each one about 4 inches (10 cm) long.

10 Hot glue the ovals to the back of the tube as wings. Let the glue dry.

BIG BUTTERFLY BEAUTY

a COLORFUL BUTTERFLY THAT WON'T FLY AWAY!

MATERIALS

newspaper	pencil	2 chenille stems
white card stock	scissors	craft glue
paint, different colors		

1. Cover your work surface with newspaper. Fold the card stock in half. Open it back up. Drop **globs** of paint on one half of the card stock.

2. Fold the card stock on the same fold again. Press down so the paint inside spreads. Unfold the card stock. Let the paint dry.

3. Fold the card stock on the same fold again. Draw half of a **butterfly** along the folded edge. Cut out the shape. Do not cut along the folded edge. Open the card stock to see the butterfly's wings.

4. Curl one end of each chenille stem. Twist the straight parts of the stems together. Glue the stems down the center of the butterfly's body. Let the glue dry.

LOVELY LITTLE LADYBUGS

TURN ROCKS
INTO ADORABLE
LADYBUGS!

MATERIALS 🔥

newspaper	paintbrushes	hot glue gun
round, smooth rock	black paint	& glue sticks
red paint		small googly eyes

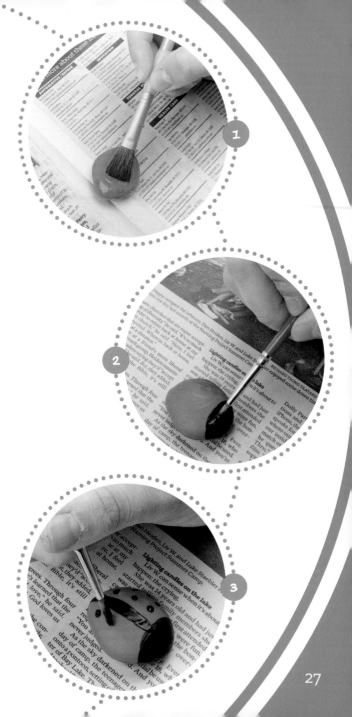

1 Cover your work surface with newspaper. Paint the rock red. Let it dry.

2 Decide which end of the rock should be the face. Paint it black.

3 Paint a thin, black line down the center of the rock. Add black dots on each side of the line. Let the paint dry.

4 Hot glue googly eyes to the face. Let the glue dry.

5 Gather more rocks to make more **ladybugs**!

GREEN GRASSHOPPER CLIPS

THESE GRASSHOPPERS CAN GO WHEREVER YOU GO!

MATERIALS

wooden, hinged clothespin

green marker

1 green chenille stem

scissors

googly eyes

craft glue

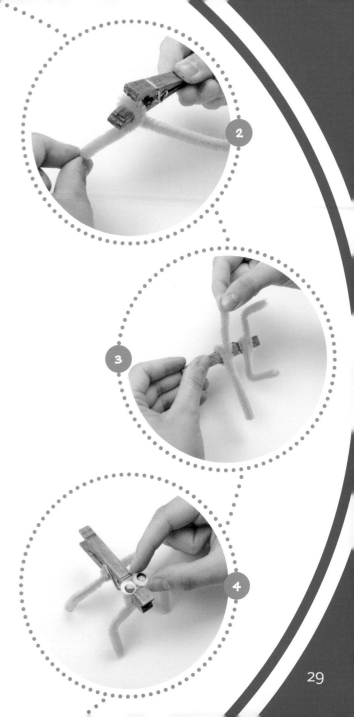

1. Color the clothespin green.

2. Cut the chenille stem in half. Open the clothespin. Wrap the middle of one of the chenille stem halves around one side of the clothespin. Bend each end of the stem to form the front legs.

3. Put the other chenille stem half through the wire circle in the clothespin. Cross the ends under the clothespin. Bend each end of the stem to form the back legs.

4. Glue googly eyes on top of the clothespin. Let the glue dry.

5. Gather more supplies and make a whole crew of grasshoppers!

CHIPMUNK PENCIL CUP

THIS CHIPMUNK STORES MORE THAN NUTS AND BERRIES!

empty can	brightly colored felt	brown, white & black felt
measuring tape	scissors	
paper	hot glue gun & glue sticks	black marker
pencil		small black pom-pom

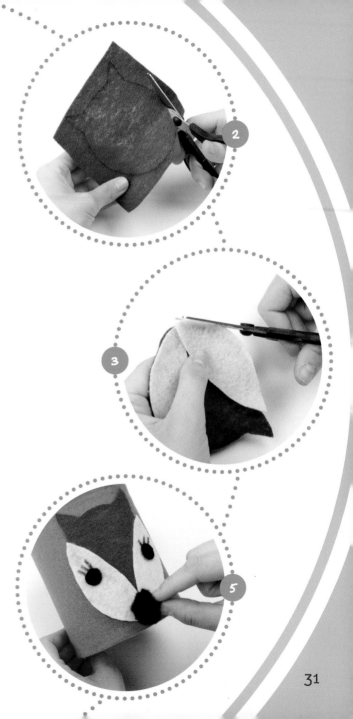

1. Measure around the can. Write down the measurement. Measure the height of the can. Write down the measurement. Cut a rectangle out of brightly colored felt using the measurements. Hot glue the felt to the can.

2. Cut an oval out of brown felt. Make its height slightly shorter than the can. This is the chipmunk's head. Include two triangles on one end for ears.

3. Cut two leaf-shaped pieces of white felt. Make each piece almost as long as the head. Glue one on each side of the brown oval. Trim the edges to match the oval.

4. Glue the face onto the can. Cut two small circles out of black felt. Glue one to each side of the face for eyes. Add **eyelashes** with black marker.

5. Glue the black pom-pom where the white felt pieces meet.

31

GLOSSARY

butterfly – a thin insect with large brightly colored wings.

eyelash – one of the hairs that grow on the edge of the eyelid.

fertilizer – something added to soil to make plants grow better.

glob – a large drop of something.

hibernate – to pass the winter in a deep sleep.

ladybug – a small, round beetle that is usually red or orange with black spots.